SALT MELTS WORDS

Tom Morton-Smith

SALT MEETS WOUND

OBERON BOOKS
LONDON

First published in 2007 by Oberon Books Ltd
521 Caledonian Road, London N7 9RH
Tel: 020 7607 3637 / Fax: 020 7607 3629
e-mail: info@oberonbooks.com
www.oberonbooks.com

A catalogue record for this book is available from the British
Library.

Cover design by Oberon Books

ISBN: 1 84002 752 5 / 978-1-84002-752-5

Printed in Great Britain by Antony Rowe Ltd, Chippenham.

Characters

The English

DYLAN SINGER, writer

NICOLA CHRISTIANSON,
translator

MIKE, publisher

ANDREW MAITLAND,
professor of antiquities

FRANCES MAITLAND,
the professor's wife

MARTHA TEMPLEMAN,
mother

MOLLY TEMPLEMAN,
daughter

SAMUEL WINCHESTER,
plague doctor

ALEXANDER BURNES,
explorer

JAMES GERARD, explorer

The Central Asians

BACHTIAR, language student

OMAR KHAYYAM,
poet and philosopher

HASSAN SABBAH, terrorist

ANICHKA, teacher

FIODOR, writer

OLGA, war veteran

YULDUZ, fish-wife

The Americans

BAILEY RITTER,
son of an oil magnate

COLONEL HACKER,
US army

LIEUTENANT DAVIES,
US army

Plus

Merchants, Travellers, US Army Privates, Salvagers and others

Four languages are spoken in this piece: English, Russian, Uzbek and French. For information, English translations of the non-English lines are printed in square brackets immediately after them. These are not intended to be spoken.

Non-Roman script has been transliterated so that the text is accessible to actors.

*With thanks to Dolya, Maftuna and Phil
for their work on the translations*

Salt Meets Wound was first performed at Theatre503, London, on 8 May 2007, with the following cast:

DYLAN Damian O'Hare

NICOLA Catherine Cusack

BACHTIAR / HASSAN / CHIEF Emilio Doorgasing

ANDREW / BURNES / HACKER Matthew Douglas

FRANCES / MOLLY / ANICHKA Rebecca O'Mara

MARTHA / OLGA / YULDUZ Ellen Sheean

MIKE / GERARD / DAVIES Jonathan Warde

SAMUEL / RITTER / KHAYYAM Sargon Yelda

Other parts played by members of the company.

Director Paul Robinson

Designer Max Jones

Lighting Design Kevin Sleep

Sound Design Richard Hammarton

Stage Manager Jason Ferguson

Deputy Stage Manager Lottie Cousins

Assistant Director Kathryn Ind

Producer Caroline Steinbeis

Act One

LONDON

1

TITLE: LONDON, 2002

Restaurant.

MIKE, big, unhealthy, eating.

DYLAN, all angles and nervous twitching, drinking water.

MIKE: Hot lamp in the face stuff? Good-cop, bad-cop?

DYLAN: Needed it spelt out – in Technicolor. The police…they
  had the pictures there but they needed me to spell it out.
  They'd been there…at the Crime Scene…but they wanted
  me…step by step…'why did I climb in the window', 'why
  hadn't I noticed something before', 'do I not talk to my
  neighbours'. Course I don't talk to my neighbours! Who talks
  to their neighbours? What sane person wants to have contact
  with the bastards next door?

MIKE: Sense of community? Companionship?

DYLAN: I'm not into companionship – not the sort that shares a
  wall. I keep one friend in every borough, I keep them well
  away from each other and I keep them well away from me.
  They said, 'We've got to look out for one another, we've got
  to talk to our neighbours.' I vomited. On the desk. On their
  recording equipment. Onto Bastard Number One's lap. It's
  just flies. I hate flies. I hate insects. Had the window been
  closed I wouldn't have to be dealing with this shit.

MIKE: But you'd have two rotting corpses next door.

DYLAN: If they don't bother me I don't bother them.

MIKE: It'd smell eventually.

DYLAN: It smells now, but only because they left the window open. That's how the flies got in. Swarming over his eyes like a horror film. And his overflowing colostomy bag. Shit and piss and flies dancing in shit and piss. How does someone get that big? Big fat fuck. I'm sorry; you're eating.

MIKE: How big…?

DYLAN: Fifty-five, sixty stone? I don't know. Too heavy to stand on his own two legs. Dying of thirst in the middle of London, how does it happen?

MIKE: And the old dear?

DYLAN: His mother apparently – though you wouldn't know to look. Tiny little thing. She never left the house – couldn't pull herself out of her son's gravitational field. What a way to spend your life – caring for your ungrateful fat sack-of-shit offspring. Some sort of fit, epilepsy, stroke, aneurysm. Caught her head on the mantelpiece on her way down. She must've been a bit of a spurter from the looks of it. Jesus. I didn't sleep last night – couldn't close my eyes without the buzzing filling my head. They obviously don't make clothes in big fat fuck size – he was wrapped in a bed sheet. Like some emperor, some Nero. My mind's on a loop. The same image over and over. I need some sleep.

MIKE: Maybe it was a glandular thing, maybe it wasn't his fault. Are you sure I can't get you a drink?

DYLAN: I wouldn't keep it down. I'd just yak all over you and you'd never get a table here again. And then where would you take all your clients?

MIKE: I only bring the big guns here – the novelists, the essayists.

DYLAN: Have you ever heard of it in England? It's an American disease and I've got Typhoid Mary next door.

MIKE: Dylan, don't…this isn't the arena for America baiting. It's not cool anymore…it's insensitive.

DYLAN: My block of flats has got subsidence. Maybe it'll sort itself out when they take the fat bastard away.

MIKE: He's still there?

DYLAN: They've got to take down the wall to get him out. And
they can't do that 'til tomorrow. I can't go back tonight – I
need to sleep.

MIKE: Have you got somewhere to…the in-laws are staying with
us at the mo, otherwise I'd…

DYLAN: Yeah, yeah. Don't worry about it. I'm sorry.

MIKE: Don't be. You've nothing to be sorry about.

DYLAN: I've messed you around enough.

MIKE: We all need a little break at the moment. We're all
uncertain. We're all a little scared. Since September…we've…
well none of us…I work in an office block for Christ's sake.

DYLAN: I don't need a break – I need to work.

MIKE: And I suppose this would be a bad time to ask you how the
writing's going?

DYLAN: What writing? I haven't written anything in…I've dried
up. Nothing inspires me.

MIKE: This is the most fertile political climate in years.

DYLAN: I'm a historian, I'm not a…commentator. I take history
and add colour – isn't that how you put it? I need a box of
crayons, not a laptop.

MIKE: The world's eyes are on Central Asia. The general public
know next to nothing about Afghanistan and…and the
other Central Asian states. People are hungry for the human
element – the culture, the history, the people. We can provide
that – it's an opening in the market. The first book you
ever pitched to me was about a Persian poet…a thirteenth
century…?

DYLAN: Twelfth.

MIKE: …a twelfth century Persian poet. That's the sort of thing I
mean. It's cultural context…it's historical…I'm not expecting
some Flashman romp…but a bit of the exotic, a bit of the

romance. We need to remind people it's not all terrorists out there but…

DYLAN: …but belly dancers as well?

MIKE: Exactly. Puffing on their sheesha. People love that kind of shit. What was this guy's name?

DYLAN: Omar Khayyam.

MIKE: Exactly. Take a trip. Clear your head. Do a bit of research on this Omar guy, see what comes from it. Disappear off to the continent, go somewhere a little less targetable. My brother's got a little place in Salzburg – absolutely beautiful.

DYLAN: I hate Europe. I'm a Londoner and they treat me like an Englishman.

MIKE: Further afield then. A beach, a ski resort –

DYLAN: He had an exercise bike. The fuck had an exercise bike. If he had ever tried to get on it the whole thing would've disappeared up his arse. How do you get like that? How do you keep it up? She must've been feeding him lard sandwiches and cake continuously. On a pension.

MIKE: Slow metabolism perhaps?

DYLAN: Where does the moment come? At what point do you get on the sofa and decide never to stand up again? And what about the sofa? They'll winch him off tomorrow and find that it's been compacted down to coal. A whole new seam of fossil fuel – an untapped resource.

MIKE: Get your mind off it. Where do you fancy? Anywhere in the world. The playgrounds of the rich…

DYLAN: I don't know. I want to go to sleep. I want to sit in my flat and not smell decay. I want to leave chicken out in the kitchen defrosting without the fear that flies have been dropping in from next door, laying eggs in my food. They throw up to eat, do you know that? All flies are bulimic. And so when they yak on my food they bring with them semi-digested fat-fuck from next door and spew it all over ready for me to eat.

MIKE: Where are you sleeping tonight?

DYLAN: I'll go round my sister's. She's got enough tranquillisers
in her bathroom cabinet to knock me out for a week.
Underneath all that, the blubber, the chip fat and mayonnaise,
he had a skeleton the same size as any man.

MIKE: Just put it out of your mind.

DYLAN: I don't put things out of my mind. I hoard. I dwell. You're
right, it's a good idea; I need to get away. My flat has been
sullied. Desecrated. How can I ever look at the dividing wall
again and not picture whale man and his symbiotic mother
rotting on the other side.

MIKE: Dylan, you're obsessing.

DYLAN: Don't use that word. I hate that word. (*Pause.*) A trip.
Yes, a trip. I need to re-evaluate. The noise in London, it's too
much. Police sirens, cars, trains, helicopters. Omar Khayyam.
He always wrote with such a stillness – a simplicity. I'd kill to
write like that. I've always wanted to travel the Silk Road. To
visit the centre of the earth. It makes perfect sense.

MIKE: Not much of a holiday though. When I said research, I
meant: in a library, a library with a private beach.

DYLAN: I should have done it years ago.

MIKE: The world was a little different then.

DYLAN: I'm not about to fly out to Kabul or hitch a ride on a B52.
I want to see the trading domes of Bukhara, the azure blue
tiles of Samarkand. I want to see the Oxus. I'll dance around
the borders of the war zone and watch the American bombers
fly overhead.

MIKE: Look at my face. This is not a happy face.

DYLAN: It was your idea.

MIKE: No, I suggested books...books.

DYLAN: Heading inland to the heart. As far from England as I am
Japan. As far from the North Pole as I am the Equator. Doesn't
that excite you?

MIKE: It worries me. This is not the time to wander round Central Asia.

DYLAN: I'm going to do this.

MIKE: God, Dylan…! Right. Just do it properly. Get yourself an Arabic speaking guide, someone who knows the area, someone who –

DYLAN: They don't speak Arabic, they speak Russian. I know someone who can speak Russian.

MIKE: Fine. Great. But do it properly. And I want you to promise me something.

DYLAN: What?

MIKE: Every morning, while you're out there, take a moment and say to yourself: 'I am not John Simpson'.

DYLAN: (*Laughs.*) I'll do that. Thanks, Mike.

MIKE: No need. Now are you okay?

DYLAN: 'Okay' is a fair description.

MIKE: Go home – to your sister's, whatever. Get some rest. Down a bottle of scotch. Try to forget.

DYLAN: I won't.

MIKE: Try. Call me next week. Let me know before you start booking tickets.

DYLAN: Thanks. I've got to go – I've got to catch a train.

MIKE: You've got my number. I never switch my phone off. If you need to talk…

DYLAN: If I ever need to talk I'll call my mother.

MIKE: That's right. Don't bring your shit to me – unless you want me to publish it.

2

TITLE: LONDON, 1912

ANDREW and FRANCES MAITLAND enter.

FRANCES is elegantly dressed.

ANDREW is a little shabbier, of the same class but a bit unkempt. He is drowning in luggage.

FRANCES: You wait here, Andrew, I'll find a porter. There's never any help around when you need it – one of the aspects of England I won't be missing. I'll be glad to leave this place behind.

ANDREW: Really? Because you seem to be bringing most of it with us. (*A suitcase slips from his grip and clothing spills everywhere.*)

FRANCES: Andrew!

ANDREW: (*Starts scrambling about, stuffing clothes haphazardly back into the suitcase.*)

FRANCES: Just put everything down and try to be a little less red in the face.

ANDREW: Sorry.

FRANCES: It's not your fault there aren't any porters. This wouldn't happen in America, they're so eager to please, and ever so polite. Americans are the politest people in the world.

ANDREW: America – it's all cowboys and puritans.

FRANCES: Oh Andrew, what a generalisation! You won't be able to say such things when we land in New York.

ANDREW: Won't you miss London even a little?

FRANCES: With it's cramped mediaeval streets and its ancient inhabitants. No, in New York the –

ANDREW: Streets are paved with gold?

FRANCES: Don't be facetious.

ANDREW: (*Pulls out a hipflask and takes a swig.*)

FRANCES: New York has been planned, intricately, intimately. Not built on the rubble of the past but on new ground, untrodden soil. Here the aromas of history seep through the floorboards, and, despite the romanticising of the past, the present always smells more pleasant. (*Notices him drinking.*) Oh Andrew – what are you doing?

ANDREW: Drinking. It'll make the journey a little more tolerable.

FRANCES: I understand. I do. But in New York…

ANDREW: A new world, a fresh page? Look, I'm putting it away.

FRANCES: Thank you.

ANDREW: Last night someone asked me why I was abandoning Britain. Abandoning. They said that America has the allure of the new; that all the emigrants will come back home once the dream has faded.

FRANCES: And what was your answer?

ANDREW: To what?

FRANCES: Why you are 'abandoning' England?

ANDREW: I told him I had found somewhere better. Not America, but you. Next to you is the only place I feel I belong – no matter how much I'm going to miss London, no matter how excited I am about New York – it all pales in comparison.

FRANCES: I would hate to think I am dragging you halfway round the world.

ANDREW: You're not. I promise. I feel its pull as strong as you.

FRANCES: We will be happy there. That is something I promise. And we will arrive in the New World in such style! I am almost as excited about the journey as I am the destination. They say the ship is unsinkable.

ANDREW: That's a relief. Though we have to survive the train journey first.

VOICE: (*Off.*) The boat train for Southampton is now boarding at platform seven.

FRANCES: No porters anywhere! We'll just have to carry it ourselves. Take one last look around. Perhaps I will miss London; perhaps I will miss London just a little. (*Exits.*)

ANDREW: (*Follows with luggage.*)

3

TITLE: SOUTHWARK, 2002

NICOLA CHRISTIANSON's flat.

NICOLA sits in the middle of the floor, draining a bottle of red wine. Her eyes weigh heavy in their sockets and she has the lethargy of drunkenness. She is bleeding from her arm.

On the floor in front of her is a goldfish, thrashing itself against the floor in a fast diminishing puddle.

NICOLA, using the sort of handheld spray reserved for delicate household plants, is occasionally spraying the fish; cruelly prolonging its life.

DYLAN enters.

DYLAN: Nicola? I'd like to say the door was ajar but... You didn't hear me knocking? I knew you were in, the lights were on. I didn't want to startle you but...I still have my key. Nicola?

NICOLA: (*Looks up.*)

DYLAN: What are you doing with the fish? And your arm – Jesus, your arm. (*Pulls out a hanky and applies pressure to the wound.*)

NICOLA: (*Winces.*)

DYLAN: You're not completely numbed then. I won't be a moment. (*Exits.*)

NICOLA: (*Sprays the fish – swigs from the bottle – looks around, unsure as to who else might be in the flat.*)

DYLAN: (*Re-enters with two glasses of water – he takes the bottle from NICOLA and presses one glass into her hand – he places the other on the floor, scoops up the fish and puts it in – he takes a better look at her arm.*) It's not so bad really. I doubt you'll even need stitches.

NICOLA: Dylan?

DYLAN: Hold this tight. (*Exits.*)

NICOLA: (*Drinks the water, seems surprised it's not wine.*)

DYLAN: (*Re-enters with bandages.*) What have you been doing to yourself?

NICOLA: You've turned my wine into water. What an annoying miracle.

DYLAN: You're dehydrated. Drink. I'll have you patched up in a jiffy. Can you tell me what happened?

NICOLA: I fell over. Into the fish tank. There's glass all over the bedroom floor.

DYLAN: I'll clear it up.

NICOLA: No! I don't want you going in there. I don't want you here. How did you get in?

DYLAN: I still have my key.

NICOLA: (*Holds out her hand.*)

DYLAN: (*Takes key from pocket and returns it to her.*)

NICOLA: You've broken the armistice. You've invaded my territory. Your being here is an act of war.

DYLAN: I've missed you too.

NICOLA: Of course you have. That's why you're here tonight. But forget it, buster, I've moved on.

DYLAN: I can see that.

NICOLA: Do you know how long it took me to get you out of this flat? Your hair in the plughole? Your fingerprints on the edge of the mirror? You look older.

DYLAN: It's been four years.

NICOLA: But you look ten years older.

DYLAN: I've had a tough week.

NICOLA: Are you getting enough exercise?

DYLAN: (*Laughs.*)

NICOLA: Why are you laughing? Don't laugh at me.

DYLAN: I should be crying. To see you like this.

NICOLA: Like what?

DYLAN: Drunk.

NICOLA: You've seen me drunk before. Many times. The first time. I've been having a party.

DYLAN: But no one came?

NICOLA: You came.

DYLAN: I wasn't invited.

NICOLA: No. But you're welcome.

DYLAN: Thank you.

NICOLA: Why are you here?

DYLAN: I wanted to ask you a favour.

NICOLA: That's rich.

DYLAN: I'm going on a trip. I need a translator.

NICOLA: You're going to Russia?

DYLAN: No: Uzbekistan.

NICOLA: I'm sorry?

DYLAN: Uzbekistan.

NICOLA: Do you have a deathwish?

DYLAN: Something we have in common.

NICOLA: I'm a drunk, not an idiot.

DYLAN: At least you acknowledge it.

NICOLA: Uzbekistan? As in: 'borders with Afghanistan'?

DYLAN: Yes. The little hand reaching out to tweak the nipple of China.

NICOLA: Are you out of your tiny little mind?

DYLAN: Maybe.

NICOLA: We're bombing Afghanistan. There are terrorists in caves and fundamentalism and guns.

DYLAN: Yes there are. But I don't want to go to –

NICOLA: What's in Uzbekistan?

DYLAN: The remnants of Persia.

NICOLA: And you need a Russian translator?

DYLAN: The remnants of the Soviet Union.

NICOLA: When else would Dylan Singer fly out to Central Asia but when we're waging war?

DYLAN: Quite possibly.

NICOLA: It's all ego. Are you going to wear a turban and try and pass yourself off?

DYLAN: Maybe. (*Pause.*) It'd be good for you. Where better to dry out than the desert?

NICOLA: Why now? What's happened?

DYLAN: I need a translator.

NICOLA: I am not the only Russian linguist in London.

DYLAN: You have to go with your instincts. (*Moves to the window.*) I've missed this view. There's smoke.

NICOLA: Where?

DYLAN: Across the river. Will you come?

NICOLA: You could've called first.

DYLAN: You would've hung up.

NICOLA: You didn't even have the decency to let me slam the door in your face. My head's not clear enough for this. You can't just turn up – that's not how normal people work. They call, put out feelers, ask people – they don't let themselves in!

DYLAN: And how would I do that? Who would I talk to?

NICOLA: I don't know. Uzbekistan? What for, research?

DYLAN: I need to get away.

NICOLA: From what?

DYLAN: From my flat, from London. I can't seem to tune in on anything. Ghosts everywhere.

NICOLA: Ghosts?

DYLAN: History. Everywhere.

NICOLA: What do you expect? It's an old city. London's built on a foundation of plague pits.

DYLAN: Not just that…

Silence.

NICOLA: So why do you want me to tag along? You haven't been a part of my life for four years.

DYLAN: I see you've found an adequate replacement. (*Pause.*) That was unfair.

NICOLA: Don't flatter yourself. You're not the only man to have ever hurt me and you're certainly not the most recent. (*Pause.*) What's this book about?

DYLAN: It's my, um…

NICOLA: Ancient Persia, right? Omar Khayyam?

DYLAN: Yes.

NICOLA: You think now is the time to –

DYLAN: Absolutely. He's a significant…he spent his days composing love poems, his nights mapping the stars, he pretty much invented algebra. He's Isaac Newton, he's John Keats and he's Islamic. We're not fighting barbarians.

NICOLA: Only a writer would think poetry is important.

DYLAN: Isn't it?

NICOLA: Contrary to whatever you may believe, very few women like to have poetry recited to them – especially halfway into a perfectly reasonable fuck.

DYLAN: What do you want me to say to that? That I apologise for having loved you?

NICOLA: No. No, I don't want you to say anything.

DYLAN: Nicky –

NICOLA: You have no right to shorten my name.

DYLAN: Nicola –

NICOLA: You have very little right to talk to me at all.

DYLAN: You're sobering up and getting angry.

NICOLA: Don't patronise me.

DYLAN: Perhaps this was a mistake. I wanted to rebuild a bridge –

NICOLA: It's been too long. (*Pause.*) I had better clean up this mess.

DYLAN: I'll do it. I said I would.

NICOLA: Don't.

DYLAN: Sorry.

Silence.

NICOLA: How would this work?

DYLAN: We'd fly to Uzbekistan in a couple of weeks. Flights to Tashkent are –

NICOLA: I have some things to sort out. I have commitments. I need someone to feed the fish.

DYLAN: Does that mean –?

NICOLA: Nothing means anything. Maybe I'll call you next week. It's getting late. Are you going back to Putney?

DYLAN: No. I can't go back to my flat. I'm staying with my sister.

NICOLA: Where's she?

DYLAN: Barnet.

NICOLA: That's a long way.

DYLAN: Yes.

NICOLA: You would have to leave now.

DYLAN: Yes.

NICOLA: Goodbye.

DYLAN: Goodbye. (*Exits.*)

4

TITLE: SOUTHWARK, 1666

The Templeman Household.

Out the window and across the river, London is burning.

MARTHA TEMPLEMAN lies in bed, floating in and out of delirium. She has the Bubonic Plague and will be dead within a day. MOLLY TEMPLEMAN, her daughter, is by her side tending to her. MOLLY's eyes have no more tears to cry.

MARTHA mutters continuously.

MOLLY: Shh, Mama. Save your words. If you must speak, pray. Please Mama, pray.

VOICE: (*Off.*) Bring out your dead! Bring out your dead!

MARTHA: (*Strains as though to stand.*)

MOLLY: That's not for you, Mama. Lie down and rest. It's a judgement, a test. This is a mysterious way, nothing more, and I trust in God's guiding hand.

VOICE: (*Off.*) Bring out your dead!

MARTHA: (*Attempts to stand.*)

MOLLY: That's not for you! Stay in bed, huddle up, rest. Let it pass through you.

MARTHA: Jonathan...

MOLLY: He's not here, Mama. We gave him over, remember? Onto the cart. Into the pit. It's a terrible sight. Bodies on bodies, no covering, no coffin. Not enough trees for coffins. I couldn't stand that, rubbing against strangers for eternity, I couldn't bear it.

A knock at the door. SAMUEL WINCHESTER enters. He is a plague doctor. Head to toe in black robes, the plague doctor's mask covers his face – birdlike. MOLLY stands back and lets SAMUEL approach MARTHA. He inspects her, looks into her eyes, feels her forehead, inspects her armpits for buboes. Done with MARTHA he turns his attentions on MOLLY. Up against the wall, he inspects her in pretty much the same way. MOLLY grits her teeth. SAMUEL takes off his mask. He holds a small posy of flowers to his nose.

SAMUEL: You need to get her out of here.

MOLLY: Will the fresh air do her good?

SAMUEL: I'm not concerned about her. She'll be dead within the day. But you need to get her out of here.

MOLLY: Can you not help her?

SAMUEL: I've smelt worse but this place definitely has it. Cart her off as soon as you can. Bring in some fresh flowers. And burn those sheets.

MOLLY: Within a day?

SAMUEL: I cannot cure this. But I can try to prevent it in you. It may already be too late.

MOLLY: Oh Lord save us.

SAMUEL: I doubt he's listening. I doubt he has ears. No hearing man could ignore the screams and prayers of Londoners today.

MOLLY: I trust in God to save us.

SAMUEL: To save us from a year of plague he sends a holy fire to cleanse our streets. What a merciful god, what a just god.

MOLLY: I can see the fire, it stretches across the horizon, the world is burning.

SAMUEL: I can feel it, even across the river. I've never known such heat in September. (*He strokes MARTHA's hair.*) What did you do for God to punish you so? The merchant's disease. Is this the cost of heathen silk and spice? It seems too harsh a sentence. And I see no silk in this house, nor spice either.

VOICE: (*Off.*) Bring out your dead! Bring out your dead!

SAMUEL: What's your name?

MOLLY: Molly.

SAMUEL: Molly, take your mother downstairs, throw her on the cart.

MOLLY: What?

SAMUEL: You cannot leave her rotting up here. She's as good as dead. Pick her up and throw her on the cart.

MOLLY: She's my mother! I need to bury her. She's not even dead. I can't let her die on a cart of corpses.

SAMUEL: Look at this place. There are no fresh flowers, you have a bowl of shit in the corner, and you are mopping your diseased mother's brow with river water. It is not inevitable that we are all going to die of this. We have survived a year and a half of this pestilence; do not give into it now.

MOLLY: This is my mother, sir, she is all I have left. If she dies then I have nothing. I would rather be dead.

SAMUEL: Easy to say, but not the slightest bit true. It is the hardest thing to resign yourself to death. The body still fights even when the mind is gone. Look at her, she sweats even now as she wrestles with the disease.

MOLLY: And she may yet win.

SAMUEL: (*Shakes his head.*)

VOICE: (*Off.*) Bring out your dead!

SAMUEL: Listen to me – you are a good and dutiful daughter. You stayed with her to the end, whispering love into her ear – that's ultimately all a human being can do. You have done enough. Take her downstairs.

MOLLY: (*No response.*)

SAMUEL: (*Puts on his mask and approaches the bed – he lifts MARTHA up and heads towards the door.*)

MOLLY: What are you doing! Don't take her! Mama! Don't take her please!

VOICE: (*Off.*) Bring out your dead!

MARTHA: Molly?

MOLLY: Mama!

SAMUEL exits with MARTHA in his arms. MOLLY breaks down, fresh tears. The fire becomes more intense across the river. MOLLY climbs onto the bed and wraps herself up in the infected sheets.

TASHKENT

1

TITLE: TASHKENT, UZBEKISTAN, 2002

Hotel bar.

DYLAN and NICOLA are sat at a table drinking coffee.

NICOLA: This place is collapsing. Have you noticed? The drains are blocked, the electricity uncertain. The furniture's falling to bits. The wallpaper losing its will to hold onto the wall. I'm not really complaining.

DYLAN: Are you not?

NICOLA: I'm striking up conversation. Someone has to. (*Pause.*) I wasn't expecting so many concrete housing blocks. Do you feel it? The fingerprint of the Soviet Union. The watchful statues and monuments that dominate the parks. (*Sips her coffee.*) This coffee is rank. I need a proper drink.

DYLAN: (*Disapproving look.*)

NICOLA: I'm not going to. I'll be a good girl – I'll stick to the coffee. It's so thick, it's like tar. I dislike hotel bars – you're always one drink away from completely forgetting where you are. And the tower blocks outside the windows don't help. Nothing has done more to bring the world together quite like concrete. And yet beneath it all you have the chandeliers in the subway, the pink-veined marble. Who thought such a bland city deserved such a beautiful underground system? (*Pause.*) Are you even glad that I'm here? I haven't been able to tell.

DYLAN: Digging?

NICOLA: A little.

DYLAN: (*Slides a beautiful gift-wrapped parcel across the table.*)

NICOLA: What's this?

DYLAN: Something to say thank you.

NICOLA: (*Opens the package – it's a book.*) Omar Khayyam.

DYLAN: I want you to enjoy this trip as much as I will. I hope you don't mind.

NICOLA: It's lovely. Thank you.

DYLAN: I wouldn't've been able to pull myself away on my own.

NICOLA: From what?

DYLAN: (*Playfully.*) Why are you digging?

NICOLA: I'm looking for the chandeliers beneath – I don't believe you're tower blocks all the way through.

DYLAN: I'm sorry – I should be showing you the sights, I certainly shouldn't be taking you to bars.

NICOLA: It'll be good for me – strengthen my resolve. Promise you'll sort out a guide tomorrow?

DYLAN: I promise.

NICOLA: Thank you. What are you running from?

DYLAN: It's nothing. I just – I've lived in London too long. There are no more virgin streets for me. Each corner triggers a memory I'd rather not have. Each restaurant, each bar, each tube station. Even if they bulldoze the building it doesn't alter the location. It still remains the place where I took my mother for her sixtieth birthday, or where I saw a tramp get hit by a BMW, or where I first smelt Amanda's hair.

NICOLA: (*Rests her hand on his.*) Hey.

DYLAN: It's been so long since I last said Amanda's name. I didn't imagine I'd be saying it in front of you.

NICOLA: (*Removes her hand.*)

BACHTIAR approaches, a little tipsy. A large body-builder of a man. It is hard to determine his age.

BACHTIAR: American?

DYLAN: What? No – English.

BACHTIAR: English! Wow. Would you mind?

DYLAN: Not at all.

BACHTIAR: (*Sits.*) I am a student of English, an opportunity to speak English with English is rare. Americans are more common but less good, teach me bad habits, sloppy diction. You are on business here? Oil?

DYLAN: Business, yes, but not oil. I'm a writer.

BACHTIAR: Really? Wow. You should write about me – I am a great character. And you are pretty lady?

NICOLA: I'm a translator, Russian linguist.

BACHTIAR: Ti gavarish pa ruski? [You speak Russian?]

NICOLA: Maya mat praishodit iz Ruskoy semi. [My mother's family were Russian.]

BACHTIAR: Ne smesheniy Uzbek s Ruskim kak mi vidim zdes? [Not a mongrel Uzbek-Russian like you find around here?]

NICOLA: Ya nastoyashaya Anglo-Ruskaya, yesli vapshe eto sushestvuyet. [I'm very much Anglo-Russian, if there is such a thing.]

BACHTIAR: Ya polnosti Uzbek. Ya ne garzhus etim, no eta tak. [I am fully Uzbek. Not that I am proud of it, but that is what I am.]

DYLAN: Didn't you say you wanted to practise your English?

BACHTIAR: I apologise. My memory is not so good. During my military service my senses were keen, my mind sharp. But time and many blows to the head have knocked any sense from me.

DYLAN: You were in the military?

BACHTIAR: Of course. The inclusive army – all tribes in one uniform. Russians, Ukranians, Balts, Uzbeks, Tajiks. But I always saw it as Russian – they were the worst, they had the teeth. They looked at us Uzbeks as though we were some desert vermin – living in yurts, with horses' milk around our lips. Wild men – and they brought us civilisation. What are you writing about? Are you writing about our corrupt leader? Our terrible poverty? Our mafia run businesses? What are you telling the world?

DYLAN: It's a book about Omar Khayyam, the poet.

BACHTIAR: I do not know this man. He is Uzbek? He is famous in England?

DYLAN: Not famous, no. Well, he was in the nineteenth century. You have no idea who he is?

BACHTIAR: No – I do not read poetry. Are you a famous writer?

DYLAN: I don't know about that.

NICOLA: He's only had one book published. Or have you churned out something else in the last four years?

DYLAN: (*To BACHTIAR.*) After your military service, what then?

BACHTIAR: I turned to a life of crime – I have to say it like this, it makes pick-pocketing sound glamorous. Perhaps I should not have said that. Please do not distrust me – I do not steal anymore; I am studying English. I steal only your language. My friend was left paralysed after the police caught him. They use rubber truncheons with steel inside. I have heard of people being boiled to death. It's becoming difficult for decent people to survive at all. You have to belong to a mafia.

NICOLA: Do you?

BACHTIAR: Occasionally. Does that frighten you? I am not proud. I work as a bodyguard for one of the mafia bosses sometimes. It is not hard. You just need to pull a mean face. I have never beaten anyone up. I cannot bear to see someone reduced to a quivering animal. Bleating and bloody. It will come to it one day. Soon. They will ask me to do something for them and it will be easier to say yes. I am a rather pathetic person I think. It is strange, to talk in a foreign language is to remove yourself from yourself. Do you understand? My wife says I do not talk enough. She says I am reticent. I am an uncommunicative language student – but I am trying to better myself – I speak English and I cannot stop. I try to speak English whenever I can. I shout it at the bellies of the American aircraft as they fly overhead. They fly low – weighed down with bombs and men. I could not be in the army again. They do not talk back, and I know they cannot hear what I am saying, but they are still more responsive than the Canadians you meet in these bars.

NICOLA: I'm surprised they're allowed to fly over Uzbekistan.

BACHTIAR: Why are you surprised? Is this not why you keep our corrupt leader in power – why you keep him rich with your monies? Are we not your strongest ally in Central Asia? A country where it is illegal to play snooker. The fundamentalists America are after include a group of anti-government Uzbeks living in Afghanistan as guests of the Taleban. I am not saying I sympathise with the terrorists, but this is not a country in a geographical sense, this is a grey area. I should perhaps not speak so openly, but my little speech is my rebellion. I feel less pathetic. And yet I am unable to say this in Uzbek. And so I am pathetic again. Do you like snooker?

DYLAN: How do you mean?

BACHTIAR: I run a little place near here where we have a functional table. I can take you there if you wish. It will not be expensive.

DYLAN: I'm not very good to be honest.

BACHTIAR: I woke up one morning and they had banned snooker. I had never even played it before. Now I am perhaps quite good. I will give you a discount because you let me talk. I do not know why they banned it – I cannot see any underlying political message in the game. Come, rebel with me. The revolution will come from the snooker halls! (*Laughs.*) I will not force you, I am unlike that, but if you change your mind I will be sat over there. Thank you for listening, people here are often too scared to listen.

NICOLA: Dasvidaniya. Beregis sebya. [Goodbye. Take care.]

BACHTIAR leaves.

DYLAN: That was very sobering. (*Realises his mistake.*) Sorry.

NICOLA: Thank you for the book.

DYLAN: No problem.

NICOLA: Right. So…how does it feel, now you're here – mixing with the natives – ushering in a new golden age of exploration? How do you see yourself? A Livingstone? A Stanley?

DYLAN: Bukhara Burnes would be a better comparison.

NICOLA: Who?

DYLAN: Livingstone and Stanley…they explored Central Africa. Alexander Burnes…he would be a more accurate…he was the first European to enter Bukhara and –

NICOLA: Stop it. Stop being so goddamn knowledgeable. It gets on my tits. (*Beat.*) Sorry.

DYLAN: It's alright.

NICOLA: It's not… I just… I could do with a drink, that's all.

DYLAN: It's okay. Can you smell that? Cinnamon.

NICOLA: I'll get some more coffee.

2

NICOLA's hotel room.

Key in the lock. NICOLA enters with BAILEY RITTER. He is a tall, clean-cut New Yorker. He has a glass of vodka in his hand.

NICOLA: Well here we are.

RITTER: Room seven. My lucky number.

NICOLA: Don't be presumptuous.

RITTER: I take it that guy's not your…or anything?

NICOLA: We're not involved.

RITTER: Okay. So…two single westerners in the exotic East; one, a tall dashing young suit with an executive position, the other…?

NICOLA: Translator, Russian linguist.

RITTER: The other a beautiful, striking, Russian linguist. Their eyes meet across six feet of empty Uzbek bar –

NICOLA: What part of Canada are you from?

RITTER: Montreal.

NICOLA: Je ne crois pas. J'ai regardé assez série-comiques pour l'identifier grace un New Yorker. [I don't believe that for a second. I've watched enough sitcoms to know a New Yorker when I hear one.]

RITTER: I'm afraid you've lost me.

NICOLA: Where do you really come from?

RITTER: New York.

NICOLA: Why lie?

RITTER: You learn, travelling as much as I do, never admit to being American. Especially to other westerners. And, now you know I'm from New York, we'll spend the rest of the evening talking about 9/11 when I'd much rather talk about you.

NICOLA: I'm sorry. (*Pause.*) Just next time pick a city a little less French.

RITTER: Is Edmonton better?

NICOLA: Much. (*Pause.*) So did you know anyone who…in the…?

RITTER: Two. Someone I went to high school with. The sister of one of my friends.

NICOLA: And where were –?

RITTER: I was out of town.

NICOLA: I'm sorry.

RITTER: Don't be. (*Pause.*) They're not martyrs, are they, the hi-jackers. They didn't martyr themselves, they martyred the location. Some people said it was a test of faith. I came to the conclusion that God is either dead or deaf.

NICOLA approaches him, downs his vodka, and kisses him, briefly but firmly on the lips. She heads for her bags and rummages through. She pulls out a walkman and two portable speakers. She plugs it in and presses play.

NICOLA: Music.

RITTER: With English lyrics! I left my walkman on a train three months ago.

NICOLA: How long have you been out here?

RITTER: Since September.

NICOLA: Oh God.

RITTER: Getting on that flight was fucking difficult.

NICOLA: Why are you out here?

RITTER: Why is anyone out here? Business.

NICOLA: What type?

RITTER: The best type: oil. My father's oil company.

NICOLA: So you're a rich-boy then? Set to inherit millions?

RITTER: We have to find the oil first. My father's landing tomorrow, otherwise I'd be out in the desert: drilling. It's so empty out there; you forget any people live here at all. And so salty, everything's covered in salt. This country has so much untapped potential – a man could make his fortune here. (*Pause.*) You?

NICOLA: Excuse me?

RITTER: And you. What are you doing out here?

NICOLA: Dylan's a writer, researching his magnum opus. He asked me to be his translator.

RITTER: That doesn't explain anything. He could hire himself a guide for less than the cost of your plane ticket. So why are you here? You're not looking for oil, you're not writing a book, how are you planning on making your fortune?

NICOLA: Dylan asked.

RITTER: It's a long way to come for someone you don't seem to like very much.

NICOLA: I had nothing better to do.

RITTER: And that's enough?

NICOLA: Sometimes.

RITTER: I expect it to be a little more complex than that.

NICOLA: Why? Why should it be?

RITTER: No reason. Prying mind. Imagination. (*Pause.*) But it is, isn't it?

NICOLA: Yes it is. (*Pause.*) It must be hard…being away from New York.

RITTER: Yes it is. Very hard. I don't like it. I suppose I must be geographically closer to it all, but I spend my days in the desert. They don't know I'm there. I'm not a target. Where I drill, it used to be a sea. It's all dried up now. You walk on seashells.

NICOLA: Don't mention that to Dylan. It's the sort of bleak romantic image that'll have him cumming in his pants.

RITTER: How long have you been here?

NICOLA: Couple of days. We're setting off to Bukhara tomorrow, then on to Samarkand.

RITTER: You'll love Samarkand. It's beautiful.

NICOLA: You've been there?

RITTER: No. I'm hoping to go, once the work eases off. (*Pulls out his wallet, finds a business card.*) The number of a guide the company uses. He'll take you where you want to go. You seen all the sights of Tashkent?

NICOLA: Been sleeping off the jetlag mostly. We went to the park.

RITTER: You stand beneath the statue of Timur? First it was Lenin, then Stalin, Marx, and now they have independence from Russia the Uzbeks cling to the only hero they have. Timur, Tamerlane. A warmonger and a tyrant.

NICOLA: As we stood beneath it Dylan's eyes glazed over and he recited a speech from *Tamburlaine the Great.* He wanted to seem spontaneous, to mark the occasion somehow, but he had been committing it to memory for about a week.

RITTER: 'Accursed be he that first invented war!
    They knew not, ah, they knew not, simple men,
    How those were hit by pelting cannon shot
    Stand staggering like a quivering aspen leaf
    Fearing the force of Boreas' boisterous blasts.
    In what a lamentable case were I,
    If nature had not given me wisdom's lore,
    For kings are clouts that every man shoots at,
    Our crown the pin that thousands seek to cleave.'

NICOLA: I don't know whether to be impressed or scared.

RITTER: What did he do to you?

NICOLA: I'm sorry?

RITTER: He must have affected you in some way for you to be in such a paradox. Wanting to be with him, but hating him.

NICOLA: Please do not use 'hate' so lightly.

RITTER: I didn't realise I was.

NICOLA: It'd been one of those 'will-they-won't-they' things. He didn't love his wife, he said he never had. And when she died, it was inevitable that he and I, well… It must have been too soon. The sudden flurry of release, being allowed to be with the one you love, instilled some guilt in him. After two months he said he didn't deserve to love me and he left. Four years later I find him nursing me back to soberness asking if I fancied a bit of a trip to Uzbekistan.

RITTER: You have very beautiful eyes.

NICOLA: In what way?

RITTER: Excuse me?

NICOLA: In what way are they beautiful?

RITTER: Just the shape, the colour –

NICOLA: Crud. You don't have to chat me up.

RITTER: (*Kisses her.*)

NICOLA: (*Receives kiss.*)

RITTER: Is this alright?

NICOLA: It's fine.

They kiss again.

RITTER: Do you still love him?

NICOLA: No.

He kisses her. They fuck.

BUKHARA

1

TITLE: THE ROAD TO BUKHARA, 1832

BURNES' camp.

ALEXANDER BURNES and JAMES GERARD, two Englishmen dressed as Uzbeks, sit to the edge of a group of about eight; travellers, merchants and others, including a local chief, who is in deep discussion with one of the travellers. It is dark and the group are huddled around a fire.

BURNES and GERARD speak quietly between themselves.

GERARD: Burnes. Burnes. Alex!

BURNES: What?

GERARD: Is he looking this way?

BURNES: No.

GERARD: What's he saying?

BURNES: He's offering us safe passage into Bukhara.

GERARD: And?

BURNES: I don't think he's the sort of man you want to be indebted to. I think our friends are keen to get us away unnoticed.

GERARD: I'm scared.

BURNES: I know. But be scared inwardly.

GERARD: I've gone cold. Clammy. I must be pale. I must be luminescent.

BURNES: We all look the same in this light. He has no reason to suspect anything.

GERARD: I think I've got my turban on backwards.

BURNES: Inwardly.

GERARD: Sorry.

One of the travellers turns to GERARD and offers him some bread.

TRAVELLER: Mana, oling. Iltimos, Olloh uchun ozgina jim bo'linglar. [Here. Eat this. And, by Allah, keep your voices down.]

GERARD: What's he saying?

BURNES: Take the bread. (*To TRAVELLER.*) Rahmat. [Thank you.]

They listen to the murmur of the crowd.

They've heard of some Firingees coming this way. He's asking for them to keep an eye out.

GERARD: Are they dangerous? Burnes, are they dangerous?

BURNES: Who?

GERARD: These Firingees.

BURNES: He means Europeans. He means us.

GERARD: I'm sorry. I don't mean to be jittery. I've been fine up until now.

BURNES: I understand. I'm scared as well. But we're close. A few days more and we'll be in Bukhara. We will be the first Englishmen, first Europeans in Bukhara.

GERARD: What about Moorcroft?

BURNES: It doesn't count unless you come back.

CHIEF: Do'stlarim, sizlar uzoqdan kelgansizlar, va sizlar mening mehmonlarim, agarda qornilaring och bo'lsa, uyalmasdan olingar. [My friends, you have travelled far and you are my guests, you are hungry. Eat, drink.]

A large bowl of shaslik is passed around the group, along with a bottle of something.

GERARD: (*Drinks.*) What is this? It's quite strong.

BURNES: (*Drinks.*)

GERARD: Is it alcoholic?

BURNES: I think it's water.

GERARD: (*Takes a strand of meat from the bowl and eats it, it is quite tough.*)

BURNES: How is it?

GERARD: Fine, really. (*Gags.*)

BURNES: Are you alright?

GERARD: Fine. I've just pulled out one of my teeth that's all. Oh God. I'm bleeding.

BURNES: Keep calm. Swallow it.

GERARD: My tooth?

BURNES: Your mouthful.

GERARD: Why are we here? Why am I here?

BURNES: Keep calm. Do you know how much pleasure they would take in killing us?

GERARD: Deep breath, James, you haven't really been dragged out to deepest Persia, you have in fact just fallen asleep in an armchair in the East India Club. Deep breath. Oh yes, another brandy would be splendid. Thank you. It's no use…I can feel blood rushing down my throat. We could turn back now, no one but you and I would know.

BURNES: James…

GERARD: I know. I know. I'm just scared. And cold. And dirty. And toothless.

CHIEF: Do'stlarim, man juda hafaman, sizlar mani yordamimni qabul qilmaganiz uchun. Man sizlarga oq yol tilayman. Yahshi qolinglar, do'stlarim. [My friends, I am sad that you will not accept my help but I wish you well on the rest of your journey. I will leave you in peace. Goodbye, my friends.]

BURNES: He's leaving.

The CHIEF is embracing all the travellers, bidding them all farewell. He approaches GERARD.

CHIEF: Hushyor bo'ling Yevropaliklarga. Ular qaerdan paydo bo'lishini bilmaysizlar. [And keep vigilant for the Europeans. You don't know where they could appear.] (*Embraces GERARD – laughs heartily – exits with his men.*)

BURNES: There. They've gone. We've survived.

GERARD: For now.

TRAVELLER: Bizga omad kulib boqdi. Mani jonim charchadi. Ozgina dam olay. [We were lucky tonight. My poor heart could hardly take it! Get some sleep.]

BURNES: Rahmat. [Thank you.]

GERARD: We can't go back, can we? It's too late.

BURNES: Get some sleep.

GERARD: I wouldn't want to even if we could. Thank you, Alex. I'm not really complaining… I just…thank you. Goodnight.

The camp settles down to sleep. BURNES is left watching the embers of the fire dissipate.

2

TITLE: THE ROAD TO BUKHARA, 2002

NICOLA sits on a dusty verge as the sun sets. She is reading her copy of the Ruba'iyat. DYLAN approaches with a bottle of water.

DYLAN: Hey.

NICOLA: Hey.

DYLAN: Water?

NICOLA: Got anything stronger?

DYLAN: (*Gestures to the book.*) How are you getting on with it?

NICOLA: I've been dipping in and out. Some of it's very beautiful. How long now?

DYLAN: About three and a half hours. We may have to consider the very real possibility of spending the night in the car.

NICOLA: He said he'd be back before it got dark.

DYLAN: The sun's already setting.

NICOLA: Then he's bound to be back soon.

DYLAN: He seemed a little under-prepared for a guide. What are we paying him for? I blame the Canadian – he took an instant dislike to me at the bar and has palmed us off with some inferior scam-monger and his clapped-out death-wagon.

NICOLA: You were being a little bombastic. And America-bashing is not everyone's favourite pastime.

DYLAN: I thought he'd've joined in.

NICOLA: You were sounding a little racist.

DYLAN: They're a culture, not a race. It's their ideas that are different, not their genetics.

NICOLA: Several thousand people died.

DYLAN: Yes. A few thousand. It's the arrogance…to canonise a single day…9/11…as though nothing had ever happened on the eleventh of September before. Well stuff had. The battle of Stirling Bridge. The Chilean coup that brought Pinochet to power. The RAF firestorm that killed 11,500 Germans in Darmstadt. The Great fucking Fire of London. Are we only allowed 365 cataclysmic historical events? It's nonsense…and it's pumped up self-importance that gives over one entire day to the deaths of 3000 people – simply because they were Americans.

NICOLA: They weren't all Americans.

DYLAN: I know. I'm just not a hypocrite, that's all. I'm not going to change my opinion overnight. (*Pause.*) Did you sleep with him? The Canadian?

NICOLA: Yes.

DYLAN: Just like that? You hardly knew –

NICOLA: Do you really want to have this conversation?

DYLAN: Not really.

NICOLA: And he wasn't Canadian – he was American. He pretends to be from Montreal so thick-headed Europeans don't start berating him for his government's foreign policy.

DYLAN: Oh.

Silence.

NICOLA: Do you want some chocolate? (*Produces a chocolate bar.*)

DYLAN: Where did you get chocolate?

NICOLA: Picked it up in Tashkent. Do you want some?

DYLAN: Wouldn't mind. (*Takes it.*) What is this? It's got Leonardo DiCaprio on it.

NICOLA: It's *Titanic* chocolate.

DYLAN: What?

NICOLA: They're *Titanic* mad – haven't you noticed? DiCaprio chocolate, Kate Winslet cola. They were showing the film on loop at the hotel. The picture quality was poor and the voices were dubbed by a single disgruntled middle-aged man.

DYLAN: (*Laughs.*)

NICOLA: What's so funny?

DYLAN: All those Edwardians fighting for air beneath the Artic Ocean, lives flashing before so many eyes, and in the last nanoseconds of brain activity the question occurs: 'how will I be remembered?' I can guarantee not one considered the possibility, a hundred years later, of being honoured in the form of a Central Asian chocolate bar. (*Picks up the book.*) The Ruba'iyat – the original, handwritten – was lost on the Titanic. One of Islam's greatest literary treasures lies at the bottom of the sea amongst the last drowned remnants of the British Empire. And what do they get in return? James Cameron. (*Pause.*) Is this what the last four years have been like? One night stands with greasy yuppie twenty-somethings?

NICOLA: Can we not start this, can we just sit here in peace, eating chocolate...

DYLAN: How old was he? Twenty-one? Twenty-two?

NICOLA: I didn't ask.

DYLAN: (*Flicks through the book.*) I wish I could see it like him. Khayyam. 'The dust under every fool's foot – Is a darling's upturned hand and a sweetheart's cheek.' But I can't. To me it's just dirt. Or dead strangers strewn over the ground. I want to see lovers reunited on a potter's wheel, the intimacy of becoming clay together. But there's none of that for me. I wish there was but there isn't.

NICOLA: You spend too much time looking at the dust. Have you ever read this book?

DYLAN: Of course I have. What a strange –

NICOLA: From cover to cover?

DYLAN: Yes.

NICOLA: Only...Bukhara isn't mentioned once.

DYLAN: (*Looking at the floor.*) Well, look at that.

NICOLA: What?

DYLAN: (*Picks something up.*) A tooth.

NICOLA: The introduction lists all the places he was known to live. There's a possibility he spent some time in Samarkand, but really we're too far north. He lived in Nishapur and Isfahan. That's in modern day Iran. And Balkh – that's in Afghanistan. Please don't think I'm suggesting we try and cross the border. We're just slightly off the mark.

DYLAN: (*Toying with the tooth in his hand.*) I wonder how long it's been here. I've read of medieval ribcages and skulls that still stick out of the ground in the ruined towns of Turkmenistan – preserved by the extreme dryness of the sand around them. Stone circles of ribs, marking the day of a long forgotten massacre as the Mongol armies hacked through the plains. Genghis Khan trying to get West, Alexander the Great trying to get East, the Russian Tsars and the revolutionaries that overthrew them striving South. No wonder this land is dust.

NICOLA: Dylan – please – I think we're in the wrong place.

DYLAN: I find it difficult to believe a learned man like Khayyam wouldn't've, at some point in his life, felt the need to see Bukhara or Samarkand.

NICOLA: To see what, though?

DYLAN: The buildings, the art and the architecture.

NICOLA: The azure blue tiles…

DYLAN: Yes.

NICOLA: The trading domes and the towers…

DYLAN: Yes.

NICOLA: Tamerlane's mausoleum…

DYLAN: Yes.

NICOLA: The twelfth century poet would have made a pilgrimage to see the tomb of a fifteenth century tyrant?

DYLAN: Well, no, obviously…

NICOLA: What are you going to do when we get there?

DYLAN: Research.

NICOLA: From what source?

DYLAN: From the atmosphere, the location…

NICOLA: And this atmosphere is still there after nine hundred years?

DYLAN: I hope so.

NICOLA: You're setting yourself up for a major disappointment.

DYLAN: The sky is still the same, the desert hasn't changed.

NICOLA: Nothing remains the same. Even the stars are in different positions now, and in the desert the dunes shift with the wind. I think you've got caught up in some nineteenth century misunderstanding. We're not in the romantic east, there are no harems and opium dens, there are no poets. I can't smell any spice in the air. The dust is nothing. The past is nothing. History's just a preamble...to now...to now, here.

DYLAN: Enough! You're right! I can't see him! This isn't how I imagined it. I knew I wouldn't be surrounded by belly-dancers and djinns. But I thought I'd get a whiff. I thought I'd catch a glimpse.

NICOLA: If you wanted the romanticised east you should've gone to Brighton Pavilion. It would've been cheaper.

DYLAN: I want people to...they have to know...it's not all beards and fanatics... I want to show people... I want to bring them something beautiful...so that they can understand where all this...the current climate...it didn't come out of the blue.

Silence.

NICOLA: If he doesn't turn up soon we may have to break out the travel Monopoly.

DYLAN: Drastic measures.

NICOLA: What? It's a great game. Let me guess – you were always the sports car.

DYLAN: (*Shakes his head.*) The top hat. (*Pause.*) Amanda – she would joke – I mean she hated chess, never got her head round it – so she always said, when he came, she would challenge Death to a game of Monopoly. Because it lasts bloody ages. And she would play Monopoly for as long as she could, keeping him busy, knowing that – for a few hours at least – the rest of us were living happy lives, free from the fear of Death. And even then I didn't love her. She deserved that.

NICOLA: What are we going to do?

DYLAN: I can't go home. I can't wake up every morning with the ghost of fat fuck weighing on my chest.

NICOLA: I'm sorry?

DYLAN: In the four years in my new flat, I haven't once fucked someone there, brought someone back, brought anyone over.

It was always just me in that flat, not the ghosts of me and someone else. But now it's no longer just mine.

NICOLA: What happened to your flat? You've never told me.

DYLAN: My neighbours died. I found their bodies next door. They had been there for some time.

NICOLA: Oh God.

DYLAN: Quite.

NICOLA: And you haven't been back since?

DYLAN: I went back once. I had to pick up my suitcase and some clothes. I had to pack. I was expecting everything to be infested with it: the smell. I expected to want to vomit. But the police had brought in people from a university. Scent experts. Because apparently every smell has an equal and opposite counter smell. It's a constant sensory tug-o-war. And the counter smell for dead people is cinnamon. Everything smelt of cinnamon. Here. (*Shoves his arm under her nose.*) Smell.

NICOLA: (*Smells.*)

DYLAN: All my clothes stink of it. (*Pause.*) I'm sorry – for dragging you out here, for being a stereotypically bullish Englishman, striding across the globe with the delicacy of an elephant gun.

NICOLA: You didn't drag me here.

DYLAN: That's kind of you to say but –

NICOLA: You're not the only person who runs away. I hide bottles. I live alone and I hide bottles. What does that say about me? (*Pause.*) We don't have to go home.

DYLAN: What would we do instead? You've made it quite clear there's no point in going on.

NICOLA: If you can't see the twelfth century here in the dust, perhaps you should raise your head and write about what you can see. The man in the hotel bar, the mafia, the illegal snooker halls, the corruption, the chandeliers, *Titanic* chocolate bars, Tamerlane's face on a bank note. Bailey, the 'Canadian', told me that he works on the bed of a dried up sea. This ocean has evaporated, leaving harbours in deserts, ships on sand-dunes, fishing communities sixty miles from water. And everything is covered in salt.

DYLAN: That sounds fascinating. I'd like to see that. I really would.

NICOLA: I thought you might.

An aeroplane flies overhead.

DYLAN: American?

NICOLA: Bombs against mountains: it's futile.

DYLAN: There are bad men in the world. Horrible people who do terrible things.

NICOLA: You do know you're not one of them, don't you?

Act Two

SAMARKAND

1

TITLE: SAMARKAND, 1082

The home of OMAR KHAYYAM.

The Ruba'iyat lies open on a table, a new quatrain is drying in its pages.

KHAYYAM sits in the middle of the floor, draining a bowl of red wine. His eyes weigh heavy in their sockets and he has the lethargy of drunkenness.

HASSAN SABBAH enters. He approaches the book and starts to read the open page.

HASSAN:
'One cup of wine is worth a hundred hearts and religions,
One sip worth the realm of China;
Apart from ruby wine on the earth's expanse
No other bitter thing exists worth thousands of sweet souls.'

KHAYYAM: Hassan.

HASSAN: Omar. It's beautiful – though somewhat misguided. Do you not have an embrace for your old friend?

KHAYYAM: What are you doing here? How did you get in?

HASSAN: There was no one to stop me.

KHAYYAM: Leave. Please. Get out. Please leave. Get out!

HASSAN: I cannot leave you like this. Drunk.

KHAYYAM: Leave me how you found me.

HASSAN: Here. (*Helps up his friend.*) You should not treat yourself with such little respect. Can I get you some water?

KHAYYAM: No. Get me some more wine. I think I will need it if I am to tolerate your company. They are looking for you. I could turn you in.

HASSAN: Maybe – if you were sober.

KHAYYAM: I could kill you.

HASSAN: You could.

KHAYYAM: How many lives would I save by stabbing you in the chest? What are you doing here? Have you come to kill me? I don't embrace murderers.

HASSAN: So my reputation has reached even the reclusive Khayyam? I am verging on infamy.

KHAYYAM: Is it deserved? Your reputation?

HASSAN: It depends on what you have heard – and who from.

KHAYYAM: Why are you here? I cannot shelter you.

HASSAN: I'll be gone in the morning. Is it so unbelievable that I may want to spend some time with a dear friend?

KHAYYAM: There is nothing I can do, nothing that could help. What influence I hold counts for nothing against their hatred of you. Who knows you're here?

HASSAN: No one. Do not worry, Omar, I would not bring Death to your door.

KHAYYAM: From what I hear he follows you everywhere else. You should not have come here. There's nothing for you.

HASSAN: Do you know how long I have travelled? Granted it is in my interest to keep on the move…

KHAYYAM: Nevertheless, I don't want a murderer in my house.

HASSAN: Is this any way to treat a friend?

KHAYYAM: You keep using that word, 'friend', as if it means something to you.

HASSAN: Is that not what we are?

KHAYYAM: I can think of a dozen more appropriate words. Murderer, terrorist. You have become something quite other than my friend.

HASSAN: I have become an executioner.

KHAYYAM: I want you out of my house.

HASSAN: Are you not going to offer me a cup of wine?

KHAYYAM: You would not take it.

HASSAN: But the offer is symbolic.

KHAYYAM: I see. You have come to convert.

HASSAN: I have come to offer you the chance to join us. I know what your answer will be, but it would seem impolite not to.

KHAYYAM: And that is the biggest insult. Well done, you are vindicated, you have come to my home and reassured yourself I cannot be turned, you can leave now, you must leave.

HASSAN: Is it wrong to want to spend time with my friend?

KHAYYAM: (*Enraged – throwing down the wine bowl in anger.*) OUT OF MY HOUSE!!

The wine bowl has smashed on the floor, red wine seeps into the dust, staining the ground.

HASSAN: (*Looks at the mess – gets on his hands and knees and picks up the shattered pieces – mops up the wine with his sleeve.*)

KHAYYAM: Leave it. Please. I'll clear it up.

HASSAN: It's fine – I don't mind.

KHAYYAM: I do.

HASSAN: (*Stops.*)

KHAYYAM: You realise I will never ally myself with you.

HASSAN: And you realise that if you do not, the day will come when…

KHAYYAM: Yes, yes.

HASSAN: But that day is not today. I do this because we are friends.

KHAYYAM: Accept the world we live in, Hassan, it is only then you can begin to alter it. Some seek compromise, others seek refuge.

HASSAN: In your books?

KHAYYAM: In poetry, astronomy, wine. Politics cannot infiltrate such pleasures.

HASSAN: There are those that fight.

KHAYYAM: How can you call it fighting? You send a man, alone, in secret, to kill his target in the most public and ugly way. And then your assassin simply waits to be torn apart by the crowd. How is that fighting? It is something else – I do not know what, but it is something else. How do you convince them? How do you convince a man to commit the sin of suicide in your name?

HASSAN: It is not in my name.

KHAYYAM: You must have a silver tongue, you must be a greater wordsmith than I.

HASSAN: I do not expect you to understand; you treasure your book, and when that isn't enough, your wine. I doubt you would die for either.

KHAYYAM: And how many times have you died for your beliefs?

HASSAN: It is the greatest honour – to martyr yourself, to stand with diamond-hard resolve as you are torn limb from limb. Allah will see your sacrifice and he will be pleased. And what is more, the crowd will see your sacrifice. Each man who joins us serves us in the best way he can.

KHAYYAM: And some are only fit for slaughter?

HASSAN: It is everything to die. Death is nothing to fear. I teach my assassins to befriend Death, to welcome him with a smile and a touch. Together they will walk into the busy marketplace, assassin and Death, hand in hand, intimates. The assassin points at he who is to die and Death complies. The crowd will then retaliate – in a belief that revenge is the last thing we want. And in the moments before, the observant will notice Death turn to the assassin and say, 'This is the price' and he will reply, 'I always knew it was'. And as he dies, with truth and peace on his face, a score, maybe two score, of those present shall be converted. It is not enough to merely kill, it is everything to die.

KHAYYAM: (*No response.*)

HASSAN: Say something.

KHAYYAM: Why? No argument can sway you. Nothing I can say will alter the fact that your Order of Assassins will kill and continue killing. What is your plan – to terrify the world into converting? (*Pause.*) I'll fix you a room.

HASSAN: Thank you.

KHAYYAM: Do you have no qualms?

HASSAN: About sending men to their deaths? No.

KHAYYAM: About having unleashed a new terror.

HASSAN: If it achieves my will, then no.

KHAYYAM: And what of the consequences you cannot see? (*Pause.*) Despite it all, I am pleased to see you.

HASSAN: Truthfully?

KHAYYAM: Perhaps equally pleased as I am afraid. (*Exits.*)

HASSAN: (*Alone, settles and approaches the Ruba'iyat, he flicks through a few pages.*)

2

TITLE: SAMARKAND, 2002

FIODOR and ANICHKA's house.

Hung on the wall is a portrait of Stalin.

Asleep in an armchair is OLGA – a mountain of a woman.

The door bursts open and DYLAN, *supported on either side by* NICOLA *and* ANICHKA, *enters. He is bleeding heavily from a gash on top of his head.* NICOLA *has a rucksack with her.*

OLGA *remains asleep.*

ANICHKA: Vot suda. Pust syadit na etot stul. [Over here. Put him in this chair.]

NICOLA: Vada yest? Palatentsa? [Have you got some water? Towels?]

ANICHKA: Ya paydu vazmu. [I'll go get some.]

FIODOR enters.

FIODOR: Shto eta? Kto etot chelovek? On tut vsyo zalel krovyu. [What is this? Who is this man? He's getting blood all over the furniture.]

ANICHKA: On turist. Evo abakrali. [He's a tourist. They got mugged.]

FIODOR: Shto tebye nada? [What do you need?]

ANICHKA: Vada, palatensa, binti. On ocheny ploh. [Some water, towels, bandages. He took a heavy blow.]

NICOLA: Na samom dele spasiba za eto. [Thanks for this, really.]

FIODOR: Ya prinesu palatentsa. [I'll get some towels.] (*Exits.*)

ANICHKA: On budet v paryadke. On v saznanie? [He'll be alright. Is he conscious?]

NICOLA: On ne savsem v sebe. [He's a bit woozy.] You're a bit woozy, aren't you?

DYLAN: It looks worse than it is.

ANICHKA: Pateryal li on saznaniye v kakoyta moment? [Did he black out at any point?] Did you black out?

DYLAN: I don't think so. Honestly I'm fine. I tend to bleed a lot.

FIODOR enters carrying a bowl of water and some towels.

51

FIODOR: Vot, palazhi eto pod golovu. Pastaraysa ne ispachkat mebely krovyu. [Here, hold this against your head. Try not to get blood on the furniture.] (*Exits.*)

DYLAN: Thank you. It's not serious – it's just a little cut. I doubt I'll even need stitches.

ANICHKA: Let me get you something to drink. (*Exits.*)

NICOLA and DYLAN burst into laughter.

NICOLA: I can't believe you chased after him!

DYLAN: I can't believe I caught him!

NICOLA: My hero!

DYLAN: Thank you, thank you. And for my next amazing feat… (*Pain.*)

NICOLA: Let me have a look.

DYLAN: It's alright – leave it.

NICOLA: Can you see anything?

DYLAN: Not beyond you buzzing around my face.

NICOLA: It wouldn't've mattered. There's nothing in it – just a spare t-shirt and my camera.

DYLAN: Where's your passport?

NICOLA: In my back-pocket.

DYLAN: It's the principle of the thing.

NICOLA: The poor man was terrified. The look on his face as he turned to see you careering down the street.

DYLAN: I don't think I've ever run so fast in my life! Or jumped so high!

NICOLA: You bounded up those steps and leapt – wrapping your legs around his chest, bringing him down.

DYLAN: He was shaking – I could feel him quiver. He was protecting his head with the rucksack – not the face, not the face!

NICOLA: And you calmly took the bag, stood up and turned away from him.

DYLAN: I was half expecting to get a knife between the shoulder blades.

NICOLA: He just lay there, rolling around. You were so gallant. Chest puffed out, strident walk. And then...!

DYLAN: Stupid flea-bitten mongrel.

NICOLA: Came from nowhere, right at the top of those steps.

DYLAN: Threw me completely off balance, bamm, bamm, bamm, all the way down.

NICOLA: (*Stifles a laugh.*) I'm sorry.

DYLAN: Don't be.

NICOLA: I won't tell anyone you tripped.

DYLAN: Thank you. Battle scars are always more impressive if people think you got them in an actual battle.

NICOLA: I doubt it'll scar. And if it does it'll be hidden in your hairline. (*Pause.*) Is she making you nervous?

DYLAN: Why would she?

NICOLA: Look at the size of her.

DYLAN: She isn't decomposing.

NICOLA: She's dead to the world. When did you realise you'd stopped loving me?

OLGA: (*Waking up.*) Kto ti? Shto delayesh? [Who are you? What are you doing?]

NICOLA: Mi turisti. Moy drug ranyen. Anichka nam pamagayet. [We're tourists. My friend here was injured. Anichka is helping us.]

OLGA: Anichka!

ANICHKA: (*Re-entering with vodka.*) Vsyo v paryadke mama. Oni samnoy. Ih abakrali. [It's alright, mama. They're with me. They were mugged.]

OLGA: Ya nehachu chuzhih v mayom dome. [I don't want strangers in my house.]

ANICHKA: Oni dolga ne zaderzhetsya. [They won't be here long.] I'm sorry. Here. Drink.

DYLAN: Thank you.

ANICHKA: Not you. Thins the blood.

NICOLA: Thank you.

OLGA: Kto etiy lyudi? [Who are these people?]

ANICHKA: Oni Angliyskiye puteshestveniki. Ya paznakomilas s nyime v gorode. [They are English travellers. I met them in town.]

OLGA: Ti privodish pastaronih v moy dom? Ne Anglichani li vi? Te katorih mi pobedili v voynu. [You bring strangers into my house? English are you? We beat you in the war.]

DYLAN: (*To OLGA.*) You have a beautiful house. (*To ANICHKA.*) Can she understand me?

ANICHKA: On govorit sho u nas krasiviy dom. [He says we have a beautiful house.]

OLGA: Da u menya krasiviy dom. Moy otets evo pastroil. Eto pamet o nyom. [I have a beautiful house. My father built it. It is a memorial to him.]

ANICHKA: Her father built it. It is a memorial to him.

OLGA: (*Opens a locket which hangs around her neck, it contains a photo.*) Vot. Papa. [There. Papa.]

ANICHKA: He was a Bolshevik revolutionary, but could not escape the purges. He died in a Siberian labour camp. She did not blame Stalin, she thought it wasn't his fault.

OLGA: Stalin bil silyniy. On ustanovil disciplinu. [Stalin was strong. He imposed discipline.]

DYLAN: What's she saying?

ANICHKA: Something about Stalin's strength. If we encourage her she will talk all night about the glory of the Soviet Union.

DYLAN: The last of a dying breed.

ANICHKA: I do not understand communism. To me, it is just another religion. But one with no gods, only prophets. This is why we cannot talk.

OLGA: Ya znayu sho vi abo mnye gavarite. Ya paka ne pepely. [I know you are talking about me. I'm not dust yet.]

ANICHKA: I want to take her and shake her. Is that wrong? I want to shake the communist blood from her bones.

OLGA: Ti privela Anglichan v dom moyevo otsa? S teh por kak ti viuchila ih yazik ti tolyko ob etom i gavarish. Angliya – Angliya – Angliya! [You bring English into my father's house? Since you learnt their language it is all you talk about. English – English – English!] (*Exits.*)

ANICHKA: My husband's mother. Joseph is hers; she won't let me take it down. Once she is dead I shall throw it away. Fiodor!

FIODOR: (*Off.*) Shto? [What?]

ANICHKA: Gde ti? Mi piyom vodku! [Where are you? We are drinking vodka!]

FIODOR: (*Off.*) Ya pishu. Astav menya v pakoye. [I'm writing. Leave me alone.]

ANICHKA: U nas gosti! [We have guests!]

FIODOR: (*Off.*) Ti mozhesh adin s nimi spravitsya? [You can handle them yourself, can't you?]

ANICHKA: Forgive my husband. He is having trouble writing.

DYLAN: Your husband is a writer?

ANICHKA: Yes.

DYLAN: So am I!

ANICHKA: You are writing about Samarkand?

DYLAN: Yes, well, we're writing about Uzbekistan as a whole – the politics, the people.

NICOLA: We?

DYLAN: Yes.

NICOLA: (*Pleasantly surprised.*) Oh.

ANICHKA: You are writing politics? You are not dangerous?

DYLAN: I don't think so.

ANICHKA: I am sorry to ask – but you must understand, we are just trying to avoid sides, it is safer that way. I am trying very hard not to have an opinion.

NICOLA: We're not dissidents or trouble makers. No one back home seems to know what's going on out here.

ANICHKA: And you're going to tell them?

DYLAN: Yes.

ANICHKA: And what will they do when they hear?

NICOLA: We're not dangerous.

ANICHKA: I've heard of British people, coming out here, trying to join up to a cause. Trying to fight.

DYLAN: Yes, but not people like us.

ANICHKA: Do you have religion?

DYLAN: I wouldn't…no, not really.

ANICHKA: It is better not to think too hard about these things – it is also better not to believe too hard. To me faith was always a self-righteous word for being stubborn.

NICOLA: Your English is wonderful.

ANICHKA: Thank you. I am self-taught. I am happier to read books in their original language, so I thought I would learn.

DYLAN: What do you do?

ANICHKA: I am a teacher. Do you like Samarkand? It is an inspiration. That is why my husband writes. I would like to say I am his muse, but it is the city, what romance there is left in it.

NICOLA: It's beautiful. It may sound strange but I'm not used to seeing turquoise. It's not a colour in London's palette.

ANICHKA: You are talking of Tamerlane's mausoleum? Yes, it is beautiful. Ironic to have such a beautiful monument to a man who would build pyramids of his enemies skulls.

OLGA: (*Enters carrying a WW2 Russian soldier's jacket – strewn with medals – points to a medal.*) Eto samoe visokoe priznaniye – Orden Lenina. Ya im pamagla vseh pabedit – Nemtsev, Amerikantsev, Anglichan! Vsya eta barba. Za chevo? Za kakoye dobroe delo mi barilis, vsyo schas ischezla. [This is the highest of all – the Order of Lenin. I helped beat them all – Germans, Americans, British! All that struggle. For what? What good cause were we fighting for, it has all evaporated now.]

ANICHKA: (*Shooing OLGA out the door.*) Ti shto delayesh? [What are you doing?] I'm sorry about her – I shall put her to bed. Davay, uhadi. [Go on, get out.]

OLGA: (*In doorway.*) Mi vas vsheh pabedili! Nemtsi, Amerikantsi, Britantsi! Mi vas vsheh pabedili! [We beat you all! Germans, Americans, British! We beat you all!]

ANICHKA and OLGA exit.

NICOLA: (*Takes another drink.*)

DYLAN: Are you okay to be drinking?

NICOLA: I'm not drinking. You're concussed: you're seeing things.

DYLAN: Biscuits.

NICOLA: Sorry?

DYLAN: It was biscuits. Crumbs. A crumb. And it wasn't that I stopped loving you – it was that I couldn't handle the idea of you loving me. We were eating biscuits…and I had launched

57

into some tirade…arms waving…vehemence and fervour…I can't remember about what…and you kissed me. Or rather you kissed away a biscuit crumb that had got caught in the corner of my mouth. You could've just told me, or dabbed it away with the tip of your finger, but you kissed it away. It was such a tiny event. So miniscule so as to hardly exist. But it was so intimate, sharing particles of food on the peripheries of our lips, and I…I don't deserve that kind of intimacy. I'm not worthy of it.

NICOLA: I don't remember that.

DYLAN: I wouldn't expect you to.

NICOLA: A crumb?

DYLAN: The smallest things…they can seem so insignificant I suppose…but repercussions…butterflies and tidal waves.

NICOLA: You do deserve it…those moments. You do.

DYLAN: (*Shakes his head, it hurts.*)

NICOLA: How are you feeling?

DYLAN: A little beaten up.

NICOLA: Will you be able to travel?

DYLAN: I can't wait. It'll be a great chapter.

NICOLA: It'll be a great book. Are you having a good time?

DYLAN: (*Grins.*) An excellent time. And you?

NICOLA: (*Smiles.*) There's nowhere else I'd rather be.

ANICHKA: (*Re-enters.*) I am sorry for Mama. War stories. She cannot forget the past. Can I get you something more to drink?

DYLAN: No, I think we're fine, thank you. We should be heading back to the hotel.

ANICHKA: So soon?

DYLAN: We have a long journey tomorrow.

ANICHKA: Somewhere nice I hope.

NICOLA: We're driving out to the Aral Sea.

ANICHKA: Why? It is not a holiday destination. There is nothing to see there. The fishing villages, the seaside resorts, they have all gone. Only the imprints of towns.

DYLAN: That's what we want to see.

ANICHKA: It is dangerous. Everyone out there is dying. The land there is dead, polluted and ravaged. Stalin worked the soil too hard and no goodness is left. You may as well say you want to visit Chernobyl, or…or…there is no other example. A ship out of water is an ugly thing, better to see them afloat – graceful.

DYLAN: But that is what I want to see; liners subsumed by sand, harbours sixty miles from shore. Doesn't that excite you?

ANICHKA: It worries me. You should not go there. I would feel terrible if I knew you were leaving me for that place. No, no – you won't go there.

DYLAN: Why not? It sounds fascinating.

ANICHKA: I don't think you realise how serious this is.

DYLAN: It's the gravity of the situation that attracts me. It's going to be the climax of my book – our book – the final chapter. A tragedy whose shockwaves hadn't reached the rest of the world. The centre of the earth. The world's dead heart.

ANICHKA: There's nothing out there.

DYLAN: Nothing to be afraid of.

ANICHKA: Nothing you can see. But the pesticides in the air, the tuberculosis on everyone's breath, the salt in the water. A thousand tiny deaths on every grain of sand.

DYLAN: A tiny death would be welcome. Unremarkable, never to be found. Never to be a dead weight on someone else's conscience.

NICOLA: (*Comforting.*) Dylan…

DYLAN: Look, honestly, thank you for all you've done. But we need to get going.

ANICHKA: I don't understand why you would want to see such a place.

DYLAN: That doesn't surprise me – what do you do when the world is ending, when the seas dry up and the leaders align themselves with ancient tyrants? You try not to have an opinion – you try not cause a commotion. It's pathetic – it's apathetic.

ANICHKA: You would have me fight? What are the options? It is either corruption or fundamentalism. I am trying to survive. What is there to fight for, other than my life and the lives of my family?

DYLAN: This is the heart of the world, and it is dead, it is dying, and your leaders and the oil companies and the religious fundamentalists are the maggots that feed on it. Doesn't that make you angry? Didn't this use to be beautiful?

ANICHKA: I wouldn't know.

FIODOR: (*Enters.*) Shto za visokie galasa? [What are these raised voices?]

ANICHKA: Fiodor…

FIODOR: Dumayu para tebe uyti. [I think it is time you left.]

NICOLA: Mi schas uydyom. [We'll be going now.]

DYLAN: I don't want to be angry, but if people know perhaps we can restore –

ANICHKA: Restore the sea? They talk of that, they talk of diverting the Siberian rivers into the desert. But that will only displace the problem, or spread it.

DYLAN: Not only the sea –

ANICHKA: I would like it if you left now.

NICOLA: Dylan, let's leave.

NICOLA and DYLAN head for the door.

ANICHKA: What kind of person is a tourist in another's misery?

NICOLA and DYLAN exit.

ANICHKA gently starts to cry – FIODOR comforts her.

MUYNAK

1

TITLE: THE FORMER COAST OF THE ARAL SEA, 2002

Fading, torn posters depicting hero-workers and a united Soviet Union under the noble profiles of Lenin, Stalin and Marx, cling to the walls like scabs.

Everything is covered in salt.

YULDUZ, weighed down with the responsibility of being the oldest woman left in town, speaks in Russian. NICOLA instantly translates. DYLAN listens.

YULDUZ: Ya nedumayu sho kagda nibud ischo budu lavit ribu. Umirayet more i vmeste snim umirayet derevnya. Nasha vsya ekonomika razrushena. [I don't think I will ever fish again. As the sea dies, so does this village. Our entire economy has been destroyed.] I'd say our way of life as well, but I don't remember it. We were tied to the sea, now it has gone we are tied to the ground. And the ground is polluted. The clouds collect what they can and disperse it evenly – it rains salt. It is everywhere; salt along the canal banks, salt covering the fields, it hangs in the air, the water, the lungs. It infiltrates our blood, and slowly, over time, replaces our bones. This crucial ingredient to life poisoning all who live here, stripping our kidneys, polluting our tears. They diverted the river, into the desert, and the canals they dug, no more than ditches. Most of the river frittered away into the sand. The Oxus: wider than the Nile, now a muddy trickle of spit. Since the nineteen-fifties the sea has depleted by seventy percent. And what are we left with? Unworkable salt marsh. It used to be temperate here, the warm breeze licking off the surf, holiday makers, fishermen. And the water, alive with carp, bream, roach, sturgeon, now nothing. When I was young we used to catch monsters. Sea creatures from the prehistoric age. But legends die when they are revealed, left to rot in the sun. They say salt is a preservative. The canning factory, you see it as you enter the town, once the pride of the Soviet Union. But when the sea began to recede and the fish stock deplete, did they shut it down? Lose face? Admit to their mistakes? They imported enough fish here to keep the factory going, from the Baltic. From the Baltic Sea! Madness. We built canals out to it. Chasing the ocean. Running after it. But eventually you have to resign yourself, to fate, to God's will perhaps. There's no future here. This is not an ecological disaster, it is the people here who suffer; skin rashes, stomach problems, problems with hearing and sight. And everyday the dust clouds come, gathering up the salt and the pesticides from the fields, and they whip our lungs and limpet onto our blood. The children are dying from bronchial disorders, the women from anaemia and the men from inadequacy. Nikto nemozhet izbavistya at soli. Vsya vada saderzhit soly. V prtovinom sluchaye ya bi predlozhil vam papit vadi. [Nobody can prevent salt. All our water is contaminated with it. Otherwise I would offer you a drink.]

2

DYLAN, alone, stares out into the wasteland before him – littered with the remnants of fishing boats and the bones of dead cattle. He picks up a stone and skims it along the sea that is no longer there.

NICOLA enters. She carries a water bottle from which she drinks heavily. Unbeknownst to DYLAN, it contains vodka, not water.

NICOLA: Hey.

DYLAN: Hey.

NICOLA: Some men are gathering in the streets. They're going out into the desert for salvage. There's an old military base on an island – apparently you can now drive to it. An old man was mending his fishing nets on his doorstep. They still feel the sea – like a phantom limb.

DYLAN: This is what we'll take back with us. Not silk or spice. Not oil or romance. But news of a dead world.

NICOLA: Well, there's a market for it. (*Pause.*) She made me feel bad.

DYLAN: Who did?

NICOLA: Anichka. Are we tourists? Atrocity junkies? I thought we were something a little grander than that.

DYLAN: Reporters? Pilgrims?

NICOLA: It's like a cemetery of unknown soldiers. It's like the shoes in the Imperial War Museum. You feel small and grateful you've never suffered so hard. But you're just a tourist, trying to feel some connection with the great tragedies of history. It's why people watch *Titanic*, it's why I'll visit Ground Zero when I'm next in New York.

DYLAN: You feel bad about paying your respects?

NICOLA: I feel bad that paying my respects feels good.

DYLAN: You shouldn't feel like that. People…we're like blood. We knit ourselves together, surrounding the injury. It's a form of protection. That's why we're here. The world needs to know. I'm a writer – I will write. There's an absence in the world and it pulled us in.

NICOLA: The Lord certainly works in unfathomable and inefficient ways. Dylan, you're not a very good writer, you're not even a famous writer. You were going to write a book about a dead poet.

DYLAN: And you changed my mind.

NICOLA: Stop looking for honourable reasons. You came out here to be closer to the war – to revel in how fucked up the world is. You came here to pine over lost civilisations and glories. To drown out your pains in a greater suffering. I understand that. I feel it too sometimes. I feel guilty that I get depressed, that I let the smallest things get at me. I tell myself repeatedly: there are people dying, there are people dying. And all I've got is a broken heart.

DYLAN: Nicky...

NICOLA: Don't shorten my name – it demeans me. I know why I'm here. Because you cut through...you make me feel something. And that could be annoyance or exasperation but...I'm not numb when I'm with you. I just want you to admit – to yourself – why you asked me along.

DYLAN: I wanted to rebuild a bridge.

NICOLA: No. You wanted a constant reminder of what a cunt you've been. (*Pause.*) I want to go home.

DYLAN: You think I'm a cunt?

NICOLA: No. But you do. Your wife died. And you saw it through. You were there for her. You stayed. You are a good man and we did nothing wrong.

DYLAN: I wasn't there for her – not in any meaningful way. I didn't hold her hand. I didn't mop her brow. She was death...she was decaying. And I couldn't be near it. I should've been like a child at her bedside. I should've been bargaining with God...instead I can...I can actually remember thinking...'hurry up'. It's the small things that would've eased her last moments. Skin on skin, wiping the crust from her eye, combing her hair...I should've combed her hair. I should've played Monopoly with her. But I was downstairs, working my way through DVD box sets, waiting for her to expire so I could be with you. I can't go home. I can't feel safe. And if I can't feel safe how can I switch my head off? Because we've all been woken out of it, haven't we? Do you feel safe there?

NICOLA: What do you...?

DYLAN: It's a simple question: do you feel safe at home?

NICOLA: No.

DYLAN: No. The fear of being mugged for my mobile phone – the fear of a prematurely released schizophrenic pushing me in front of a tube train – the fear that, as I look at a plane overhead, my looking will cause its engines to explode – the fear that something like New York will happen in my home town. How can you be calm in a world like that?

NICOLA: Better to drown out your guilt? Because all this makes your actions seem so insignificant? I think it's time to go home.

DYLAN: I can't... I...

NICOLA: Why not?

DYLAN: Because of the ghosts! Because of fat-fuck and Amanda and you and me and everything I've ever done! It's all there – poised, waiting.

NICOLA: And you haven't brought it with you? You think there's a limit to how much emotional baggage you can take on the plane? Just one little carry-on you can fit in the overhead compartment – nothing more. You're an idiot.

DYLAN: Don't talk to me like I'm a –

NICOLA: You think you can take all this back with us? You'll just discard it. And another four years down the line you'll be back where you started. You pick up causes like the rest of us pick up colds. How is this any different?

DYLAN: Coming from someone who chose alcohol above all else –

NICOLA: That's not true. I chose you. And you fucking...ran off...beating yourself up so you had some wounds to lick. I can understand you wanting to torture yourself but did you mean to hurt me? Was that your intention? Did it even occur to you? Or was that just a consequence you couldn't see? I'm not saying I haven't made mistakes. But at least my heart is full, you try so hard to keep yours empty.

DYLAN: Emptiness? You think that's what I want? No, that's not what this is. There are trawlers and row boats and yachts and cruise-liners and frigates and battleships and canoes and submarines and paddle-steamers and pedaloes: at rest. Stillness. The salt no longer suspended in water but at rest. The world is a storm. This is the eye.

NICOLA: This is nothing.

DYLAN: For the first time I have a subject worth writing about. I have a cause. I have a need. Can't you see? Why can't we share this? This is everything. This is you and I alone in the silence. No baggage. No history. No future. Just present. You and I – present and correct. (*He pulls her toward him and kisses her passionately.*)

NICOLA: (*Pushes him away.*)

DYLAN: What is that? You taste...you taste of vodka. (*He looks at the bottle she is holding.*)

NICOLA: Water.

DYLAN: Give it to me.

NICOLA: No, it's mine.

DYLAN: What are you doing to yourself?

NICOLA: I'm drinking. It makes your company a little more tolerable.

DYLAN: You can't do this.

NICOLA: I can do whatever I like, Dylan. It's called free will.

DYLAN: It's from the past – you don't have to have that here. You can let it go. We're out of the loop, doesn't that mean anything to you? You don't have to let the past control you – it can't touch you here.

NICOLA: Why? Why is this place any different?

DYLAN: Because this is all irretrievable. This can never be fixed. There will never be a seashore here again. There will never be holiday resorts again. There will never be fish. There will never be families. We are standing outside of time. The past has finished with this place and whatever we do will have no effect on the future. There are no more consequences, dominos or repercussions. There is only stillness. This is a conclusion. The only part of history where history stops. Put down the drink. I can't sit back and watch you self-destruct.

NICOLA: This place isn't dead. People still live here.

DYLAN: Where there's life there's hope?

NICOLA: You think this place needs an Englishman to come out here and pronounce the time of death? We need to go home.

Silence.

DYLAN: I'm going back into town. I want one last look around before we head off. You stay here. Enjoy your drink. I won't be long.

DYLAN exits leaving NICOLA alone with her bottle.

A dust storm rises on the horizon.

REBIRTH ISLAND

1

TITLE: REBIRTH ISLAND, THE ARAL SEA, 2001

A playground, rusting climbing frames, slides and swings.

The US Army have set up a base camp here and swarm over the playground. Soldiers are hunched over satellite phones, looking over blueprints, swinging on the swings. Two soldiers are wearing full bio-warfare suits and are being hosed down.

COLONEL HACKER prowls around preoccupied.

LIEUTENANT DAVIES is keeping everyone in check.

DAVIES: Is everything set up, private?

PRIVATE 1: Yes, sir. Just waiting on the Colonel's go, sir.

PRIVATE 2: Sir, all the houses have been ransacked. Same as the military base, sir.

DAVIES: Thank you, private. (*Notices a soldier sat on top of the slide.*) Hey! Get your ass down from there! Let somebody else have a go. Let's get this thing moving. Where's the Colonel?

PRIVATE 3: Over there, sir. And sir...?

DAVIES: What?

PRIVATE 3: He seems a little preoccupied, sir.

DAVIES: What are you saying, private?

PRIVATE 3: He seems somewhat melancholy, sir.

DAVIES: Go play on the swings, private.

PRIVATE 3: Yes sir!

DAVIES: Colonel?

HACKER: Yeah?

DAVIES: We're just waiting on your go, sir.

HACKER: Has someone evaluated the base?

DAVIES: Yes, sir. Risks of contamination are minimal but we did find some live spores. Rather than use explosives, and risk stirring up anything that may be buried, we thought a straightforward fire would be the best option, sir.

HACKER: Any signs of activity?

DAVIES: The base has been ransacked, as have all the houses and shops around here, but it seems restricted to metal piping and electrical wires as far as we can tell, sir.

HACKER: Let's hope so, lieutenant.

Pause.

DAVIES: Sir?

HACKER: What?

DAVIES: We're still waiting on your orders, sir.

HACKER: Burn the fucker down. To the ground. That's what we came here for, wasn't it?

DAVIES: Let's start this thing, private.

PRIVATE 3: Yes, sir! (*Exits.*)

HACKER: Within a year, a few months maybe, this will no longer be an island. And anybody will be able to walk up here, grab what remains, and start cultivating his own brand take on the finest biological weapons of the Soviet Union. We knew about this facility a decade ago, Stalin's pet science project, and it's only now we're out here to clear up the mess.

DAVIES: With due respect, Colonel, the Russians claimed to have decommissionized this base, neutralising any threat, sir.

HACKER: But there are still live spores in the ground.

DAVIES: Yes there are, sir.

HACKER: It just makes you so goddamn incensed. (*Pause.*) When was the last time you sat in a swing, Lieutenant?

DAVIES: I couldn't say, sir.

HACKER: When I was growing up we had a tyre swing in the backyard. About that same sort of time the Soviets were experimenting with the most terrifying diseases known to man. The tiniest alteration of the cellular structure and the Bubonic Plague becomes as contagious as the common cold. God knows how many rats and rhesus monkeys writhed and died in this place. God knows how many scientists coolly and calmly plotted the deaths of millions. AIDS, Ebola, Anthrax – all of which they weaponized, or attempted to weaponize here. And it would be cheap, and it would be devastating. How do you calmly manufacture that kind of terror?

DAVIES: They were bastards, sir.

HACKER: They were that, lieutenant.

A great fire begins to burn on the horizon, the same as we saw in London (4).

PRIVATE 1: She's burning up, boys! She's burning up!

All the soldiers gather to watch the fire in the distance, scrabbling for the best vantage points. Only one soldier (PRIVATE 2) does not. He is manning one of the satellite phones and is getting an important message through. The rest of the soldiers are whooping and hollering.

PRIVATE 2: Colonel? I think you should listen to this, sir.

HACKER: What is it, private?

PRIVATE 2: It's New York, sir. Something's happened in New York.

2

TITLE: REBIRTH ISLAND, THE ARAL SEA, 2002

NICOLA is sat on the swings, just coming round. DYLAN crouches next to her, rubbing her back.

Throughout the scene NICOLA looks increasingly unwell.

DYLAN: Hey there, sleeping beauty, how are you feeling?

NICOLA: Crud.

DYLAN: You've been out quite a while. You finished off the bottle.

NICOLA: Yay me.

DYLAN: How's your head?

NICOLA: How's yours?

DYLAN: Throbbing a little.

NICOLA: Throbbing a lot.

A small group of SALVAGERS enter.

SALVAGER 1: Dostingiz qalay? [How is your friend?]

SALVAGER 2: Vaqtingizni o'tqizmang, u baribir sizni tushunmaydi. [Don't waste your breath, he can't understand you.]

SALVAGER 1: U faqat mani ovozimni tushunadi holos. [He can understand the tone of my voice.] (*To DYLAN.*) Uning ahvoli tuzikmi? [She is hungover?]

DYLAN: She'll be alright. Thank you.

SALVAGER 1: Man buni uyga qizimga olib ketyapman. Biz sizga haloq etmaymiz. [I'm taking this slide home to my daughter. We will not bother you.]

The SALVAGERS go about dismantling the slide, chatting amongst themselves.

DYLAN: I don't have any coffee. They boiled up some tea earlier but it was so salty I didn't think it would do you much good. We have no common language but they seem pleasant enough. I think we amuse them, we're novelties. And I think they're grateful for the extra storage space.

NICOLA: What are you talking about?

DYLAN: Our new found friends. They're out here for salvage.

NICOLA: I can't think straight.

DYLAN: You're shaking. You're burning up.

NICOLA: Every cell in my body is drunk, I feel like I'm dismantling.

DYLAN: Why do you do this to yourself?

NICOLA: I have no rose tinted glasses – I have to make do with beer-goggles. (*Pause.*) They were heading out to an abandoned military base. Is that where we are?

DYLAN: The base is about half a mile up the road, this is the little community that sprung up around it – just as abandoned. These guys come here a couple of times a year – stripping out the copper wiring, loading up their cars with scrap metal.

NICOLA: You said we were going home.

DYLAN: No I didn't.

NICOLA: You waited for me to get paralytic and kidnapped me.

DYLAN: You were unconscious – I couldn't well leave you there.

NICOLA: You knew I wouldn't come out here with you sober.

DYLAN: Don't make it sound so manipulative. I was just joining the dots. You were in no position to have any say. That's not my fault.

NICOLA: (*To SALVAGERS.*) Kto ta iz vas gavorit pa ruski? [Can any of you speak Russian?]

SALVAGER 2: Nemozhka. [A little.]

NICOLA: Shto eta za mesto? [What is this place?]

SALVAGER 2: Zapushenaya vayenaya baza. [A military base. Abandoned.]

NICOLA: Shto oni zdes delali? [What did they do here?]

SALVAGER 2: Neznayu. [I don't know.]

SALVAGER 1: U nima dedi? [What is she saying?]

DYLAN: What are you saying?

SALVAGER 2: U faqat bilmoqchi, ular shetda nima qilishganini. Hammasini. [She wants to know what they did here. At the base.]

SALVAGER 1: Unga aytkinki, biz qurol yasagan edik holos. [They were building weapons. Tell her that.]

SALVAGER 2: Oni izgatavlyavali aruzhiya. [They built weapons.]

NICOLA: Kakie vidi aruzhya? [What kind of weapons?]

DYLAN: What are you saying?

NICOLA: The empty sea not enough for you? The ruined lives and livelihoods? The life expectancy of thirty-eight not shocking enough?

DYLAN: I'm just following things through. Looking for that natural conclusion.

NICOLA: For the book?

DYLAN: Yeah.

NICOLA: Life doesn't work like that – it doesn't come in chapters. It overlaps – it bleeds into itself. They say that weapons were built here.

DYLAN: So?

NICOLA: This is a military base, isolated – we're not talking a factory floor and assembly lines of Kalashnikovs. We're talking weapons programmes.

DYLAN: Nuclear?

NICOLA: I don't think so.

DYLAN: Then…what?

SALVAGER 2: Amerikantsi bili zdes v proshlom gadu. Ani sazhgli vskladi. Mozhet bit ani vzyali aruzhya. [The Americans were here last year. They burnt down the warehouses. Perhaps they took the weapons.]

NICOLA: Kto libo zabolel li posle payezdak takova roda? [Has anyone ever got sick after one of these trips?]

SALVAGER 2: Kak vi dumayete bolen? [What do you mean sick?]

SALVAGER 1: Nima? [What?]

SALVAGER 2: Hammani ahvoli tuzikmi? [Has anyone ever got sick?]

NICOLA: Ktoto kagda libo umer? [Has anyone ever died?]

SALVAGER 2: (*Laughing.*) Vse balniye! Vse umirayut! [Everybody's sick! Everybody's dying!]

NICOLA: You wanted to find your natural conclusion? You wanted to find the heart of the world? Here it is. A biological weapons factory. And we just strolled into it – not even a gas mask between us. What is that? In your eye? Is that a glint of excitement?

SALVAGER 3 enters.

SALVAGER 3: (*To the other salvagers.*) To'htah usha – ahlat qilish, undan ko'ra menga yordam bergin. [Stop messing around with that slide and come and give me a hand.]

SALVAGER 1: Bir daqiqa. [In a minute.]

SALVAGER 3: Yoq – hozir. [No – now.]

The SALVAGERS exit. Silence.

NICOLA: Dylan…we have to leave. We have to leave now.

DYLAN: You're in no state –

NICOLA: We've got to get out of here.

DYLAN: I'm not ready. It's not finished –

NICOLA: There is no finish. There is no revelation to take
home. This place isn't a secret – it's just ignored. There's no
natural conclusion to anything. As sure as there's no natural
beginning.

DYLAN: There has to be meaning.

NICOLA: This is becoming an obsession.

DYLAN: Don't use that word. I hate that word.

*SALVAGER 1 enters with an oil barrel on a trolley, unloads it, and
exits.*

NICOLA: What will happen? What do you see happening?
We go home with news of the rotten core of the world and
you shame the West into peace? And your past failings are
outweighed by your present good? The world is shaped by
bad men –

DYLAN: Like Hassan Sabbah.

NICOLA: Who?

DYLAN: A childhood friend of Omar Khayyam – the granddaddy
of all suicide bombers, the old man in the mountain. You can
see his influence in everything now. Khayyam was stillness.
Sabbah was chaos. And I can't see Khayyam in anything.

NICOLA: But you are not a bad man. You don't need a cause
– you don't need to make a difference. You just need to kiss
the crumbs from your lover's lips…you just need to hold their
hand as they die.

DYLAN: But I…I…didn't…

NICOLA: It is the tiny acts of good men that make a difference.

DYLAN: Look at me – I've been romanticising death. Why is
death more romantic than a glass of wine, a beautiful woman
and a sky full of stars?

SALVAGER 2 enters with an oil barrel on a trolley, unloads it, and exits.

NICOLA: Stop looking for patterns – patterns will always appear. Because the world is pretty shapes. A salt crystal is beautiful, a ship at rest on a sand-dune is beautiful, a disease on a microscope slide is beautiful. Look at me. Look me in the eye. You have made mistakes. You cannot drown out a mistake. You cannot run away from it. You can only live with it.

DYLAN: Perhaps…perhaps we should go home.

The SALVAGERS enter. SALVAGER 1 is pushing another oil barrel on a trolley. SALVAGER 2 gives him a hand unloading it.

SALVAGER 3: Moshinani qaliti olginda va qochaylik. [Get the car keys and let's get out of here.]

SALVAGER 2: Vi mozhite li mne pazhalusta otad klyuchi at mashini? [Could you please hand over the car keys?]

NICOLA: They want the car keys.

DYLAN: What for?

NICOLA: What do you think for?

DYLAN: That's not oil in those barrels, is it?

NICOLA: No.

SALVAGER 2: Pazhalusta dayte mne kyuchi mashini. [Please give me the car keys.]

DYLAN: I don't think –

SALVAGER 3: (*Pulling a gun.*) Kalitni uzat. [Hand over the keys!]

DYLAN: Whoa! Hang on. Just a minute.

NICOLA: (*A coughing fit starts.*)

SALVAGER 3: (*Pointing the gun at NICOLA.*) Siz mani unga o'q otishni hohlaysizmi? Siz yahshi ko'rgan qizingizni o'lishini kormoqchimisiz? [You want me to pump her full of lead? You want to watch your girlfriend die?]

SALVAGER 2: Bu juda zarurmi? [Is this really necessary?]

SALVAGER 3: O'chir ovozingni. Ularni yana so'ra. [Shut up! Ask them again.]

SALVAGER 2: Pazhalusta otdayte nam klyuchi. [Please give us the keys.]

DYLAN: (*Takes keys out of his pocket.*)

3

TITLE: REBIRTH ISLAND, 1972

Laboratory.

A dissection table is set up.

A tray of surgical implements to one side, glinting menacingly.

A rhesus monkey in a cage to one side is battling with the final stages of disease.

It beats itself against the side of the cage, unable to escape its fate.

Slowly and shudderingly, the monkey curls into a final painful ball and dies.

The final reflexive twitches dissipate.

4

TITLE: REBIRTH ISLAND, 2002

The laboratory has been cleared but for a few lockers along the wall. The walls are slightly smoke damaged. NICOLA lies in the middle of the floor. She is having trouble breathing and the sweat runs from her. She scratches at her armpits. She is battling with the final stages of disease. DYLAN is overturning lockers furiously – frantically - desperately, all to no avail. Nothing useful remains. Anything he finds is burnt or melted. DYLAN – with a sharp pain in his head – falls to his knees.

NICOLA: (*Coughs and wheezes.*)

DYLAN: (*Pulls himself somewhat together and crouches down beside her – he lifts a water bottle to her lips.*)

NICOLA: (*Drinks – coughs – spits it out.*)

DYLAN: (*Sniffs the water – realises it's vodka and throws it down in anger.*)

NICOLA: (*Lays her hand on him to calm him down.*)

DYLAN: You're burning up. You're running with sweat.

NICOLA: With some luck it'll refill the sea.

DYLAN: (*Failing to hold back tears.*) This isn't…I…it's so…where does it hurt…how does it hurt…does it hurt? (*Looks into her armpit.*)

NICOLA: Please don't.

DYLAN: There must be something – something that can help.

NICOLA: A little glowing green vial marked 'antidote'? (*Laughter that falls on silence.*)

DYLAN: 'Sorry' doesn't seem anywhere near adequate.

NICOLA: It still wouldn't hurt.

DYLAN: I'm sorry. I tried to catch them, I tried to chase them down. They had loaded the barrels into the back of the car. Everything's burnt – everything's charcoal.

NICOLA: They said that Americans had been here last year. That they'd burnt down the warehouses.

DYLAN: Why?

NICOLA: To cleanse, I suppose. A cleansing fire.

DYLAN: It didn't fucking well work, did it?

NICOLA: They weren't just out here for a children's playground, were they?

DYLAN: I don't think so – no. (*Pain in the head.*)

NICOLA: Dylan?

DYLAN: It's nothing.

NICOLA: (*Places her fingers in DYLAN's hairline – she removes her fingers and they are covered in blood.*) You're bleeding.

DYLAN: It doesn't matter.

Silence.

NICOLA: I think you should leave.

DYLAN: I'm not going.

NICOLA: The more time you spend here –

DYLAN: This isn't about me.

NICOLA: I want you to go home.

DYLAN: Home? What's at home? A future populated by the obese and run by incompetent Americans? No. I know where I'm supposed to be. (*Pulls her close to him.*) Look…look…I'm holding you. I'm mopping your brow. I'm combing your hair. I'm holding your hand. I'm here for you.

NICOLA: Thank you. (*Pause.*) I'm scared.

DYLAN: I know. (*Pause.*) The bastards didn't even leave us the travel Monopoly.

NICOLA: If I had to spend eternity next to any one person…

DYLAN: (*Smiles.*) I never really understood Khayyam's fascination with dust. But if you think of how we shed our skin continuously, we leave our dead cells every place we visit. And our dust fuses with the earth we walk on. And now… now…this is you and me…intimacy…becoming clay together.

NICOLA: I can smell cinnamon.

DYLAN and NICOLA wrap themselves up in each other.

A plane flies overhead.